What did people say they liked the most about grandma?

How are things been with dad since grandma is no longer around?

What music did grandma liked to listen to the most?

Do you remember grandma's favourite flower?

What did grandma do a lot that made you laugh?

Did you have a nickname for grandma?

What type of drink did she like the most?

Did grandma like any sport and if she did, was she good at it?

What was the nickname grandma gave to you?

Do you remember what favourite dress grandma liked to wear?

What was grandma's favourite snack to eat?

How did you feel when grandma was getting buried?

_____

_____

_____

_____

_____

_____

_____

_____

_____

_____

_____

_____

_____

_____

_____

_____

_____

_____

_____

What did grandma say she liked the most about you?

Do you remember what favourite shoe grandma liked to wear?

What do you talk to mom about after grandma's death?

How have your friends supported you after grandma's death?

Write down grandma's favourite food?

If you could change something about how you said goodbye to grandma what would it be?

What do you talk to dad or grandpa about after grandma's death?

_____

_____

_____

_____

_____

_____

_____

_____

_____

_____

_____

_____

_____

_____

_____

_____

_____

_____

What did grandma and you like to do during the summer season?

What did grandma and you like doing the most together?

How do you feel about grandma not being around anymore?

_____

_____

_____

_____

_____

_____

_____

_____

_____

_____

_____

_____

_____

_____

_____

_____

_____

_____

_____

What would you like to tell grandma that you didn't get a chance to say to her?

_____

_____

_____

_____

_____

_____

_____

_____

_____

_____

_____

_____

_____

_____

_____

_____

_____

_____

Have you been feeling differently without grandma being around?

What did grandma and you like to do during the spring season?

_____

_____

_____

_____

_____

_____

_____

_____

_____

_____

_____

_____

_____

_____

_____

_____

_____

_____

What did grandma and you like to do during the winter season?

What gift did you give to grandma that she was really happy to receive?

_____

_____

_____

_____

_____

_____

_____

_____

_____

_____

_____

_____

_____

_____

_____

_____

_____

_____

What did grandma say about the afterlife?

What did you wish you could have said to grandma more often when she
was alive?

_____

_____

_____

_____

_____

_____

_____

_____

_____

_____

_____

_____

_____

_____

_____

_____

_____

What did grandma and you like to do during the fall season?

Are you still doing all the things grandma taught you to do?

What did you promise grandma you will continue to do when she died?

_____

_____

_____

_____

_____

_____

_____

_____

_____

_____

_____

_____

_____

_____

_____

_____

_____

_____

_____

_____

How are things been with your siblings since grandma is no longer around?

_____

_____

_____

_____

_____

_____

_____

_____

_____

_____

_____

_____

_____

_____

_____

_____

_____

_____

What did grandma say you should do when she died?

Write down your favourite memory of grandma?

_____

_____

_____

_____

_____

_____

_____

_____

_____

_____

_____

_____

_____

_____

_____

_____

_____

_____

What does grandma's voice sound like?

What favourite snack did grandma get or made for you?

When grandma was ill at the hospital or at home, how did it make you feel?

_____

_____

_____

_____

_____

_____

_____

_____

_____

_____

_____

_____

_____

_____

_____

_____

_____

What would you like grandma to know about in the afterlife that you are proud of doing now?

_____

_____

_____

_____

_____

_____

_____

_____

_____

_____

_____

_____

_____

_____

_____

_____

_____

_____

What funny story did grandma tell you that made you happy?

Made in the USA
Monee, IL
17 May 2022